Lessons in GRACE, MERCY *and* FORGIVENESS

Adopting a Drug Baby

PETRA COLE

xulon
PRESS

To my daughter Sally, who always chose to love and find the good in Jay. She was the perfect sister for him and continues to be a wonderful daughter to me.

Also, to my sister Anne for her unwavering support and encouragement to get my story on paper. Thank you; writing was the perfect way to heal!

Acknowledgments

First, I want to thank my sister Anne for prompting me, over and over, to write this book so others could read my story. She was a great and wonderful aunt to Jay, and still is to Sally, the two I am writing about. She also knew my frustrations. She has been able to laugh with me over circumstances that, at the time they happened, lacked the humor they deserved. My sister has been my support, my go to, and a keeper of reality in my life.

I also want to thank my husband Paul, for hanging in there with me through times that were difficult with Jay, for loving my daughter Sally as his own, and giving me room in life to deal with issues as they arise. You are an amazing man Paul Cole. I am so glad you are in my life.

My friend, Sue, took the time to read my story and edit out all my unnecessary commas. I didn't realize how many commas I tend to use and how many times I change tenses. It's nice to have such an intelligent friend; thank you.

My friend, Tracey, helped me with sentence structure and bringing shape to my story. She's the one who spent hours at the computer making this book actually come together. Her understanding of the publishing process has made this really happen. Thank you also, Tracey, for your time spent in prayer.

My life-long friend, Trudy, also encouraged me and helped me through prayer and reading as I went. Thank you for all your years of committed friendship, and for being my traveling partner.

Table of Contents

Introduction

I am not a writer. Writers are creative people who can say something to draw in their readers. I am simply a person with a story to tell, a life to share. This book is mainly for those who have adopted a drug baby, or know someone who has. My story is about my two children, about tough experiences, great joys, humor *(after the fact),* and God's immeasurable grace. Grace is a word best explained by experience. Grace is a word I now understand and cherish.

This story intentionally lacks chronological order. I am writing as each memory comes to mind, one flowing to the next as thoughts naturally do.

Prologue

Psalm 37. 1 "Delight yourself in the Lord and
He will give you the desires of your heart."

Today is just the kind of day where one's mind runs adrift. My memories begin as I sit and prune flowers, pick vegetables to eat as well as freeze, have another couple of peaches (far better than a teaspoon of sugar), and I daydream. Usually my daydreams are of the past, what I wish I could change, what I am so thankful for, and all in all how very blessed I am. My life hasn't been easy, nor has it all been hard, but a comfortable mixture of the two.

I loved my childhood and would readily repeat it many times over. My high school years were, for the most part, also pretty good. I wish I would have had more confidence in who I was and who I could have been in some areas but I didn't and it cost me a good reputation. But many of us dealt with this problem and we all survived. All in all I had the most wonderful upbringing and now realize what a gift that is. However, this story is not going to start with my early years;

rather, it is about the discoveries I made in my adulthood and the maturing process I went through, much in part through parenting. It's a journey I often take through my mind and have decided to put on paper.

We adopted a little boy, who unbeknownst to us was a drug and fetal alcohol syndrome child. The process of raising Jay was full of challenges great and small, but through it all, the Lord was faithfully teaching each one of us about His grace, mercy and forgiveness. I am convinced a significant part of being a mother is the daily opportunity we are given to learn from our children, as the Lord uses them to refine our character, making us more like Christ.

My goal is to share the lives of two very special children and the road we traveled together with the hope that it may help someone else along the way.

Chapter 1

Jay

"Oh what a beautiful morning, oh what a beautiful day...Who could be more blessed than we were, to have a son we call Jay!"

If you can imagine all the energy cells of ten small children combined into one little boy, then you can begin to visualize my son Jay. He was such a beautiful child from his freckles, his little nose, sparkly eyes, right down to his long legs. He was extraordinarily coordinated; even his doctors commented on this. His young mind never stopped imagining, creating, and planning. As hard as I tried to stay one step ahead, and just when I thought I had, he would skip a step and jump two and I loved him.

He presented such a challenge. I would never know anyone who could make me angry more quickly, or bring me to tears faster. I learned from him as well and found just how much I needed Jesus to give me guidance. Looking back there are so many changes I would have made if I could have foreseen and comprehended what Jay had been through. I don't know too many people who wouldn't like to correct a thing or two in their lives, but I would've loved to have had more knowledge and wisdom while raising Jay.

Jay was not your average foster child. He was the second one my husband and I had taken in that year. Jay had a gift, and his gift was receiving and extending forgiveness. If he got into trouble and was disciplined, instead of sulking, he would throw his arms around us, say he was sorry, and the day went on as if nothing had ever happened. He smiled like there was never a reason to do otherwise. I picture him now, with that silly grin of his. Inside he must have known I found him irresistible.

Chapter 2

Remembering

Psalm 86:15 "But You, O Lord, are a compassionate and gracious God, slow to anger, abounding in love and faithfulness."

J ay was only three years old when we agreed to bring him into our home. He hardly had any hair on his head, as his mother, due to their living conditions, was always battling head lice. He was all eyes, with a big smile that spread across his face. There was very little adjustment time as he seemed to fit in wherever he was. Whether this was a learned behavior after seven foster homes in one year, I never knew, but he was the master of making do.

Our first few days were fun. We went shopping for clothes, took several showers, met the neighbors, and ate. He came with two unmatched shoes on his feet, little girls' underwear, and a noxious urine smell in his clothes. At three, he still wet the bed so we bought a few more sets of sheets to make life easier.

Jay was a handful as it appeared he knew every swear word that existed, some of which I'd never heard before! Our first serious training came in exchanging swear words with acceptable words. Thinking it would be easiest if the new words started with the same sound as the swear words, we came up with terms like "phooey," instead of the 'f' word; "shoot," instead of the 's' word, "holy cow," instead of 'hell' and so on. I gave him three warnings a day, since he was three, and any swearing after that resulted in discipline. Types of discipline were anything from sitting in the corner, no dessert, a spanking, washing his mouth out with soap, or going to bed early. Usually he did pretty well, most often catching and making the correction himself; we were really proud of him! He was not only adorable, but so smart. As many parents discover, the type of discipline had to be varied; there was never just one that worked consistently.

The first time he was given a time-out in the corner, I discovered his amazing imagination. In getting him situated I told him he needed to sit quietly and think about what he had done so he could remember not to do it again. Before long, Jay was making a "choo-choo" sound, followed by naming all the animals that were in the train he was "watching go by on the wall." His little head was counting the train cars carrying the animals as they were heading to their new home at the zoo. Jay saw it all in his little mind and told the whole story as it happened, completely forgetting why he was sitting in the corner. As far as he was concerned, the only reason he was there was to use his imagination! It was pretty much the same when he was sent to bed early, unless that meant missing a cartoon on our little television. There was never a type of discipline that remained effective more than once or twice; he definitely had very short term memory. Though I came to understand this later, at the time it was very frustrating.

I began to dream of all the possibilities for his future. I prayed for him daily hoping he would learn to understand who God was and wanted to be in his life. But most of all I had a little boy who needed me and I came to realize I needed him as well.

Being a foster child, Jay was required to have visits with his birth mom. His dad was not in the picture as his birth mom did not know who he was. At first, his visits with his biological mother were short and usually held at the Foster Care Department building. As time went on, she was allowed to take him "home" for overnight visits. After each of these visits, he would come back to us foul mouthed, smelly, and wearing clothes that were not his. Back to square one. I quickly came to detest the visits and could not understand how any organization could allow a child to be put in the situations Jay was subjected to, let alone require it on a regular basis.

One time he even returned with cigarette burns on his arms, yet the mandated visits continued. I often wondered why they said the system was for the good of the children. I certainly never saw any benefit for Jay, nor did I hear of it for others. Our experience revealed hurting children who became more deeply wounded each time they were returned to the same, unchanged parents again and again. It was heart breaking to witness and a process I still do not agree with or understand.

One of the weekends while Jay was away on a "home visit," we had our adult Sunday school class over for a barbeque. We were all sitting out on the lawn eating and laughing when we looked up and saw Jay coming down the street. Wearing only little girls' underwear, and unmatched shoes, the standard apparel for each return, he walked up in his matter-of-fact style. Without hesitating, he looked at the grill and loudly exclaimed, "Ah hell; not more hamburgers!" Make no mistake, he had everyone's attention! As a young "mom," my mouth dropped open not sure what to say. I quickly swooped him up, hugged him closely and headed him in for a shower! Once again we discussed what appropriate language was and then rejoined the rest of the crowd outside. This was the beginning of a variety of humbling occurrences that would come.

One such time I remember like it was yesterday. Jay had pushed me beyond my limits and I really lost my patience. Taking him to the bedroom, I explained the punishment and then spanked his little bottom. As soon as I finished, he stood there crying, then threw himself into my arms and told me in between sobs how very much he loved me and how sorry he was he hurt me and asked me to please forgive him. After we'd both stopped crying we spent the next couple of minutes laughing as we healed together. Forgiving and being forgiven have irreplaceable, healing value in our lives.

Chapter 3

Sally's Arrival

Psalm 57:10 "For great is Your love, reaching to the heavens; Your faithfulness reaches to the skies."

Within a few months of Jay's arrival, we received another call from the Foster Care Department asking if we would like to have Jay's younger sister with us. Though our house was small and we didn't have the "required" room, they wanted to keep the children together and decided they would make an exception. We jumped at the chance and Jay's little sister arrived the next day.

Sally was nine months old when she came to us, with very curly blond hair. Jay was immediately very gentle and caring; we watched an amazing bond take place. Her mother didn't know if she was Jay's half or full-blood sister. Sally wasn't interested in talking, but in spite of her young age, she walked everywhere very quickly. I soon discovered what a challenge it was to keep up with her!

Our first experience came when shortly after she had arrived we were all outside working in the yard. We lived on a corner, so there was a street on two sides of the house. A car horn started honking, which we took little notice of until we realized Sally was missing. Though she had been right beside us just moments before, we ran around the house and found her standing in the middle of the street! So thankful she hadn't been hurt, but feeling like irresponsible people unable to manage a small little nine month old "baby," we scooped her up to return to the yard. From that point on we set up very strict boundary rules, intended to insure nothing like that would ever happen again. However, we soon realized the error of our ways in thinking we could anticipate her next move or her speed!

Not a month later, we found her on the roof of our house reaching down to pull things out of the gutter. In the midst of a project, my husband had left the ladder unattended and Sally went right up! She had no fear whatsoever, while I felt buried in it. When she was safely in my arms I was finally able to stop shaking. We immediately agreed Sally could never be out of our sight for any length of time…ever!

Jay was very protective of her and loved her dearly. In time, the tables would turn and Sally would become Jay's protector. The two of them were very close and it was fun to have them together in our home. They were the last of eight or nine children their biological mother adopted out. Sally never had the desire to find her siblings, but as he got older, Jay wanted to know about them. I helped him search for information, but every effort came up empty.

Jay immediately became protective of Sally and we watched an amazing bond take place.

They took my heart from the very beginning!

Chapter 4

Life with Two

Proverbs 12:18 "Reckless words pierce like
a sword, but the tongue of the wise brings
healing."

For the most part, Sally was Jay's opposite. She was a thinker, not a reactor. She never left a project uncompleted. Where Jay's personality and behavior were more random and unpredictable, Sally was very purposeful. She also tended to be quieter.

However, their mutual love of the outdoors, excitement of daring discoveries, the competition of who could get the dirtiest, or the joy of any other competition for that matter, made them the best of friends. Their great imaginations provided hours of creative play!

They slept in bunkbeds in a small room that also held our freezer and a make-shift closet. Since it was originally the back entry into our house, we installed a special lock on the outer door to keep them safe. Other than the required parental visits with their biological mother, we felt like our little family was doing quite well. We soon discovered we had a small adjustment to make regarding the bunkbeds however.

Jay never wanted Sally to fall asleep before he did, so if her eyes began to close, he would lean over the top rail and throw things at Sally to keep her awake. We warned him several times about this, but when he was determined, nothing else seemed to matter. One evening after hearing a crash, we ran into their room and found Jay on the floor. Having fallen out of bed in the midst of throwing something, he looked up at us with wide eyes and said, "Well, I think this was punishment enough, don't you?!" Though we had to visit this again in the future, for a short while, the memory of falling seemed to keep him from leaning over his bunk.

Our visits to the laundromat were always an adventure I dreaded. Usually I took an assortment of things such as balloons, books, blocks, and gum to occupy our time while waiting for the washer and drier to complete their cycles. Both Jay and Sally had great imaginations, so we rarely lacked creative ways to pass the time.

One particular day as we were playing "keep the balloon off the floor," another lady entered the laundromat and proceeded to put her clothes in the washer. Having too many clothes to put in one machine, she let out an expletive. Before I could stop him, Jay was right beside her, pulling on her dress, saying, "Lady, we don't say 'damn it;' we say 'dog-gone-it' instead!" The look on her face was priceless! Jay walked away and returned to our game having made a lasting impression. Oh if only I could be so bold to encourage others, without casting any judgment! Life with this child was a ride at times I wanted to slip off of, at least long enough to catch my breath!

I was always so thankful when the machines had finished their cycles and our clothes were finally finished. When I heard the last dryer click off, it was like hearing the prison bars close behind me and I was finally free on the outside. It was one of those days I was especially thankful to be free, when the wind caught Jay's balloon as we were running out the doors. Up and up it went, slowly disappearing. Jay exclaimed, "There it goes, up in the sky…(dramatic pause), surely it's going right up to heaven…(repeat dramatic pause), well, at least God won't be bored anymore now that He has my red balloon to play with!" My son felt he had made a real contribution to God's playtime. I was thankful the Lord instilled curiosity and beautiful imaginations into the minds of children and for giving Jay an extra dose of both!

Jay adored Sally, helping her in any way he could. One of his self-appointed tasks was talking for her. She would point at something and say, "Uh," and immediately Jay would interpret for her. "Sally wants that doll," or "Sally wants that book," or whatever else Sally might want. We realized we had to put an end to that, or we were concerned she would never see a need to use words on her own. Sitting at the dinner table not too long after we told Jay he could no longer speak for Sally, she shocked us all. She pointed across the table and uttered her usual, "Uh" several times before realizing no one was paying attention to her. Not to be ignored, she opened her mouth and clear as day said, "Pass the butter, please." The room was deafeningly quiet as the rest of us simply stared at her with our mouths open. Our little girl could not only talk but spoke clearly with good manners! She never got away with much after that but her cleverness has always impressed me!

Though she'd been potty-trained since she'd joined us, there were still occasions when we were somewhere too far from a bathroom for her to make it there in time. One day when she was around three, we were all on a picnic. She came up and told me, "Mommy, I have a tricky bottom!" I thought, "Really; this should be interesting!" Sally continued, "…and my tricky bottom forgot to tell me it had to go potty!" Darn those tricky bottoms; what's a girl to do!? She always had an amusing way to phrase things. Talking with her a couple years later, Sally told me, "I suppose I will be one of those gabby women when I grow up!" Imagine that concept at such a young age.

Chapter 5

School

*Psalm 38:22 "Come quickly to help me, O
Lord my Savior!"*

School brought another new dimension into our family,
adding new authority figures and many humbling occasions for me as a mom.

We lived just a few blocks from the elementary school
where there was also a preschool. I thought a couple days
each week in preschool would be good for Jay to learn how
to properly interact with other children. He was four years old
at the time. It only took a couple of days before I received a
phone call from the teacher.

She began the conversation saying, "I would like to talk
to you about Jay's black eye." Jay had never been a fighter,
so my mind was taking off in all different directions. The
teacher continued, "I'm sure you realize your son is a leader,
don't you? Well, today he met his match. A little girl in the

class didn't want to change games as Jay had instructed the others to do, so she decked your son when he insisted they play the game he had chosen." The little girl became Jay's heartthrob. She would be just about the only one who would stand up to Jay and win.

The following year, within a few days of school beginning, I again received a phone call. This time his teacher shared with me that Jay wanted to run the classroom because he thought "he could do a better job." She invited me to come in for a conference. Though I thought to myself, "What? A conference this soon? Are you kidding me? Can't you take care of this?" I quietly said yes and went in. I'm happy to say I was so glad I did. His teacher was very observant and I was pleased at the suggestions she had for keeping him challenged and respectful of authority in the classroom. We discussed various methods of discipline and set a plan for maintaining consistency both in the classroom and at home. I highly respected her and her input, especially as time went on.

I was beginning to notice that Jay rarely took responsibility for his actions and seemed to always have a handy excuse ready. Most of them were clearly off the wall and a real stretch of the imagination. Things just mysteriously "showed up" in his pants pockets. He would say he was sure he'd been told he could take the eraser that belonged to the child beside him. Or, he was certain I'd said he could have four cookies, not just one. He was always confident he was not the one at fault.

Jay was in the first grade and loved everything about school, the kids, his work, the teacher and learning. School was a place he received a lot of attention. One day Jay had misbehaved one too many times in his classroom and was sent to the principal's office. Jay was told about the rules he needed to remember and that he, the principal, wanted Jay to be responsible and follow them. After Jay left his office, the principal called to let me know what had taken place. Believing that Jay needed to realize there was an authority figure at school, I went in and signed a form giving the principal permission to spank Jay if necessary. He said his plan was to give Jay another warning next time, using the added visual of bringing his paddle down loudly on his desk while explaining that if Jay had to visit his office again the desk would be his bottom. Later the same day Jay did in fact receive the visual warning, as the principal once again tried to emphasize the importance of Jay's need to obey. The principal called and reported Jay's reaction to the visit, stating that he thought the visual had been "quite effective;" since Jay's eyes had been "quite large," the principal was sure he'd gotten the message.

I must admit I was anxious for Jay to get home so I could hear his interpretation of the demonstration. Not long after, I heard him coming down the street, singing at the top of his lungs, clearly very happy with life. I was a bit confused. When he came in the door, we did our usual hugs and I asked how his day had been, "Did anything new or different happen today?" He told me no as he started to walk away, then abruptly turned around and with great excitement told me, "Today I visited the principal, and mom, he was whipping his desk!" Hmm, that was not exactly the meaningful lesson we were hoping for!

I called the principal the next day and we started back at square one. In reading back through my journal from that season of life, I noticed that I had actually recorded my prayer following that event. "Heavenly Father, please gift me with an imagination like Jay's, so I can handle him as well as he handles me." I had to laugh!

The class Halloween party was another new opportunity for Jay. All the kids, dressed up in their little costumes, headed out for recess before the party began. I got a phone call from Jay's teacher telling me about their day. She reported that Jay had stayed behind in the classroom and chewed all the bubble gum that was supposed to be given to each student. The note in his pocket when he got home said, "No points for Jay today; he ate the gum for our game!" When I confronted him about his selfishness, he responded, "Mom, after I chewed the first piece, I figured out there was going to be one piece missing for the party. So, instead of making someone go without a piece of bubble gum, I chewed them all!" He was completely sincere in his belief that he was truly thinking of the others. Not once did it occur to him that he was the one who should have gone without a piece of gum during the game!

This was just another moment I struggled to understand how his brain worked. At this time there was still no information available regarding the effects the mother's drug and alcohol use had on the unborn child. As studies began to surface years later, I was saddened to see proof of the thoughtlessness of our society toward those who don't yet have a voice. Apart from the Lord, people are so self-absorbed, while others pay the price.

By the end of first grade, Jay was reading very well. He loved books and I was so pleased. He also enjoyed spelling and loved the challenge of learning to spell "big" words. I began to see light coming under their bedroom door at 5a.m. and find him sitting up in bed surrounded by books. Of course the problem was he and Sally still shared the room and we all needed more sleep! On the positive side, Sally loved to have Jay read to her and in the process she learned to read at a young age as well.

Second grade was every bit as exciting for Jay, if your definition includes being well acquainted with the principal. I grew accustomed to mid-day phone calls to inform me of each current "incident" involving Jay. On one particular day the call was rather heated.

In Jay's defense, I need to preface this incident with the fact that I had always cut the children's hair, and that apparently made it seem like a natural, helpful thing to do. The little girl who sat directly in front of Jay had beautiful, long, blond braids. She shared with the class that after school, her mom was taking her to get her hair cut. Jay informed her that he could cut her hair "for nothing," and "save her mom some money!" He assured her he knew how to cut hair because his mom cut hair. Somewhere, in the course of their conversation, the little girl agreed to let Jay do what he "knew how to do." Jay then proceeded to cut off each pigtail, at its base, which to make matters worse started above her ears, leaving two completely bald spots in the middle of her head! In retrospect, I can actually understand why the mother chose the language she used to express her opinion in the heat of the moment. Hopefully, all these years later, she and her daughter can look back on the incident with laughter. In spite of recalling they went to a professional in an attempt to repair the damage, I've apparently blocked the image of the little girl's hair after that. I do still remember the look of abhorrence on the mother's face, the teacher's face, the principal's face and the little girl's face, who was standing there holding two long braids in her hands while sobbing. I'm certain my face fit right in, though Jay, once again oblivious to the consequences of his actions, seemed pleased with his accomplishment.

We were often uncertain whether to laugh or cry with this boy; he frequently gave us opportunities for both. One evening I was giving him a practice spelling test and one of the words was "seat." He spelled it "sete." When I questioned his spelling reminding him the class was working on "ea" words, he said, "I am really confused! Is this the "sete" of a check, or the "seat" like my bottom?" I explained the word he was thinking of was "receipt!" Thankfully that cleared his confusion up in time for him to spell the work correctly on his test the next day.

Jay, Sally and I went shopping for school clothes for Jay. We were in the middle of a large department store where the children had been told to stay right beside me at all times. It wasn't five minutes before Jay was missing. I really didn't give it much thought as I knew he could likely still see me, but when he didn't respond to my calling his name several times I sought help to find him. After many people were brought into the search, he was found in the middle of a clothing rack. He was afraid he'd be beaten for causing trouble so he'd chosen to remain hidden. There was still so much I had to learn about this little boy who had been in so many different environments in his short life. While Jay tragically had past experience with being "beaten," it was a completely foreign concept for me to even consider. At that point, we sat down and talked about a "special family word," that we would use as our "emergency" word when I needed him or his sister to respond to me right away. If they did not respond, I explained there would be discipline, but assured him he would never be beaten in our home.

As became his "normal," he quickly forgot the previous incident, repeating it the next time we were out shopping. This time he included Sally in his adventure. When both children were missing and not responding to my calls, I once again gathered help to search. Though normally not one to panic, I was getting close when I heard, "Psst, Mom, we're in here. We have the perfect hiding place, but don't tell anyone!" What's a mother to do; why hadn't I thought to look in the center of the clothes rack? In order to survive my inventive, creative children, I had to find humor in these situations. Thankfully, laughter comes quickly now, each time I look back on that season of life!

Sally gave us many reasons to smile. I remember the time I picked her up from preschool, and she announced she had a new friend named Jennifer, whom she loved, "just like I love Jesus Christ!" Whoa, that's a lot of love!

Jay brought his homework home from school and read one of the questions out loud. "Do you think all snakes are bad?" Jay wrote "No." I asked him what snakes were good and he said "Garden snakes and Water snakes." When I asked why he chose those, without hesitation he said, "Well, Water snakes kill any fish that try to bite you while you're swimming!"

**Every first day of school had to be documented;
they looked so adorable.**

Chapter 6

Witnessing Grace

*Ephesians 1:7-8 "In Him we have redemp-
tion through His blood, the forgiveness of sins
in accordance with the riches of God's grace
that He lavished on us with all wisdom and
understanding."*

P rior to coming to us, Jay had been passed around to so
many people within the Foster Care system, I don't
believe he could even begin to comprehend the meaning of
the word, *security*. With my family background revolving
around complete security and unconditional love, it was hard
for me to imagine what Jay's life had been. For Jay there
were no "dependable certainties," whereas that's all I'd ever
known. Perhaps that's why God chose me to be this young
child's mother; I learned so much about *grace*, God's grace
and Jay's grace.

Not long ago I was awakened by my dear husband Paul because I was crying in my sleep. I'd been dreaming of Jay as a little boy when he went through a period of time when he was repeatedly hiding food under his mattress. I couldn't fathom why he was obsessed with storing food; in our attempt to stop the behavior we finally disciplined him for it. In my dream, the realization came to me that instead of disciplining him, I should have made a peanut butter and jam sandwich with him every night to heal his fear of "running out of food the next day." In the same dream I came up with a creative idea for how I should have responded when we discovered he had stolen something. I concluded I should have made him return the item to the owner, and then taken Jay to the store to buy what he thought he needed. In my dream I was trying to correct the training moment I had missed with Jay. In retrospect, rather than discipline, I believe he needed to be given processing tools to help him make healthy choices. After my husband wakened me, I think I shed more tears of guilt for failing Jay in those moments.

As parents we all make mistakes. I can never remember Jay being mad at me, even if he'd been disciplined and we discovered later something wasn't his fault. If he were still living, I would ask him to explain his ability to forgive and move on. Whenever I apologized he would just hug me and it was forgotten. The blessings he gave to me are ones I look back on with awe. Being an avid picture taker, with hundreds of pictures from their childhood, I only have one picture of Jay when he wasn't smiling!

One of the best moments of my life came when my husband and I sat in court waiting to find out if Jay and Sally would be returned to the birth mother. I had been emotionally trying to prepare myself for losing them, while praying to the Lord would allow us to keep them. That day the judge asked their mother their birthdates but she didn't know. He asked the name of their father but she didn't know. As the questions continued she was not able to give an answer, then all of a sudden she stood and told the judge, "I would like them to be given to the couple taking care of them. If they will adopt them, I will sign the papers to give them up." I couldn't stop my tears; I was so eager to sign the papers and give them our last name! The days and months after the court date were fast and furious as we began the adoption process. We jumped through all the necessary hoops and within a few months, both Jay and Sally legally became ours.

As soon as we were officially a family of four, we climbed onto the fast track to find a new job out of the state. Our intention was to take Jay and Sally as far away as possible from their painful history, planning to begin a new joyful one of our own. I envisioned us as the "perfect" family: two perfect children, two perfect parents, with a couple of perfect dogs. I think all of us imagine we can be the best of the best, never repeating the mistakes of others, or of our parents. We were going to be the most incredible family in the state.

In my dream world I actually imagined popular magazines doing features on our family, including pictures from our photo-shoot of course!

This was to be a very short-lived dream; *perfect* just wasn't going to be the word to describe us. But then, *perfect* really isn't all it's made out to be, and we would have missed the excitement of our roller coaster ride!

Chapter 7

Moving

Psalm 29:11 "The Lord gives strength to His people; the Lord blesses His people with peace."

We moved to a small town on the coast of Southern Oregon. My husband took a principal position at the school where he also taught a couple of classes. Jay was in a combined class of first, second, and third grade students. Since we lived quite a way out of town we decided to enroll Sally in a preschool class where she could have some playmates.

It was wonderful returning to the state where I was born; though it was a different area, it felt like "home." Jay had two new loves in school, math and science. He would come home and explain why there was a night and day; how the world traveled around on its axis; why we had snow and rain...he was a little sponge taking it all in. We were pleased to see his first report card with an *excellent* in spelling, *satisfactory* in almost all other areas, with the exception being the area of self-discipline and respect for school property. The *needs improvement* summarized this elusive area of his life. His quick temper would flash, but we were thankful it dissipated as rapidly as it flared.

We grew a large garden, acquired two golden retrievers, three hamsters (all named after famous composers), and a garden snake. The garden snake was a surprise pet the children took great delight in naming and calling each time we went out to weed the garden. Who knows how many different snakes their "pet" really was, but they would call it by name and "it" would actually appear!

Jay was trying to show he had become responsible and asked if he could pick up the mail after he got off the school bus. We had a very long, steep driveway which concerned me, knowing he would have his backpack and maybe other things in his hands. He eagerly convinced me he could get the job done correctly, so Jay became our personal "mail boy." I would see him walking up the hill to our home waving the mail in his hand, a true sign of victory. He would bring it into the house, lay it on the table and proudly announce, "Another successful day!"

One morning after the children left for school, I had an errand to run in town. As I drove down the driveway, I noticed a piece of mail Jay had dropped the day before. I stopped to pick it up and discovered it was a fairly large check we'd been expecting. That afternoon I showed him the check and explained that maybe we needed to wait a bit longer before he took on the responsibility of getting the mail. I was surprised by how devastated he seemed to be over losing his job. We agreed to wait a few months, and then try again.

When the designated day arrived, he reminded me it was time to give him another chance. Since the weather had turned cold I tried to convince him it would be better to wait until Spring, but Jay was determined to prove he could be responsible. In spite of snow falling, Jay faithfully brought *all* the mail home each day.

I often watched for him to come up the hill when I knew it was time. One particular day, I heard the dogs barking, which was unusual. I looked out to see Jay holding the mail inside his coat, pressed close to his chest. The closer he got, the more excited the dogs became and then I noticed he had blood on his face! Concerned, I ran out of the house and grabbed him in my arms, but he just said, "Don't worry Mom; I didn't let go of the mail. I have it all right her in my coat, safe!" He had slipped on the ice and fallen in the snow. "My face hit the driveway, but I didn't let go of the mail!" He was so skinned up it took weeks to heal, but he had proudly proven himself responsible. I cried myself to sleep that night thinking of my brave, determined little boy.

In the warm weather the kids considered the hill along one side of the house a tremendous bonus for their playtime. It was steeper than I should have been comfortable with, but at that point I hadn't yet learned to think like my children! One day Jay and Sally took our red "flyer" wagon and hauled it to the top of the hill. I heard screams that brought me running to the door in time to see a streak of red racing by with two little heads sticking up just as they were about to hit the top of a second hill. It was too late to do anything other than hold my breath and hope I would still have two children after the crash. Somehow in the final moment of the descent, the wagon turned over, both kids went flying, jumped up and were ready to go again! I ran out hollering, "Wait, wait, WAIT; this is not safe!" Oh, but it was fun! On the next trip down the hill there were three of us in that wagon. With my longer legs I was able to slow the wagon down enough we didn't crash but still had a terrific adventure. It was great to be a kid again!

On one particularly hot day, the kids and I decided to go to the river to swim. Preparing for our trip, we put the hamsters in their cage and without thinking I put the cage on the dining room table. The kids and the dogs (my life guards) piled into the car. After a wonderful day cooling off in the water, and enjoying our picnic lunch, we headed home. Not once had I given any thought to the change of the sun's direction during the day, until we walked into the house. There was one of our hamsters, lying absolutely still in his cage. Mercy! With the hot sun shining directly in the window where I had placed the cage, I realized I had fried our poor hamster! The children were beside themselves, pleading with me to try to save him. He was their "favorite!" (at that moment anyway). I ran cool water over the hamster to try to revive it, tried drying it off with the hair dryer while pumping his little heart area, all to no avail. I had to pronounce the little guy dead.

I could only hope my children would mourn for me in such a dramatic way when I died. It was very impressive! To console two broken hearts, I found a small box, lined it with fabric, and with both children and all living pets, we held a funeral service. Such sweet things were said about the "faithful" pet who "always loved us" and "was never selfish with the other hamsters." It was a rather lengthy service but never has a hamster been put into the ground with greater care, marked grave and all!

One evening, Jay decided he was old enough to run away. He wasn't leaving because he was angry; he was just "old enough" as he said. We asked him what he needed to take and all he really wanted was a sandwich. We reminded him he couldn't cross the road at any point and he agreed. We talked about the coyotes, bears, and other wild creatures in the area. He was good with that because he was sure he could climb a tree. I thought maybe he would be gone five or ten minutes before returning, after all it was dusk and there were wild animals out there. So, off he went with his peanut butter sandwich, a coat, and some chocolate milk. We stood at the door and said goodbye, told him how much we'd miss him, reminded him how much we loved him, as he confidently walked away. We rushed to the window to watch as he went down the driveway and turned to walk in the ditch along our country road. We waited for what seemed like a long time, discovered it had only been ten minutes, but decided it was time to go check on our son.

When Jay had come to the spot where he needed to cross the road in order to go any farther, he sat down and put out his thumb to hitch-hike. Mercy! My husband picked him up and asked where he wanted to go. Jay decided home would be a good place. Thankfully my brave little wandered returned!

Little did I realize, God was preparing me for a life of watching my son wander. It was a heart breaking time of hoping he was alive, praying for a word of encouragement, and seeing the Lord perform the miraculous. Jay would teach me what it meant to be on my knees before God, shedding tears that would be held by Him. My faith would be tested, tried, and found to be vital to my sanity.

After an afternoon of gardening and running their feet through the dirt, resting on the front porch was a favorite option!

Chapter 8

Character Building Stories

*Psalm 25:4 "Show me Your ways, O Lord,
teach me Your paths..."*

Sally and Jay had a wonderful relationship; but Jay, like many big brothers tend to do, enjoyed teasing Sally unmercifully. There was a time when Jay took her favorite doll and was taunting her with it, while refusing to give it back. After many attempts to reason with Jay, Sally went into her room, unscrewed the handle from her popper-push toy, returned to the living room and Jay, and whacked him on the head. As he grabbed his head, she quickly reached down and recovered her doll. It was quite amusing: no fight, just action. She is pretty much the same today; she thinks things over, then takes action.

Easter morning, I awakened to a scream that left no question; something terrible had happened! Jumping out of bed, I raced to the living room where Sally was standing by the open front door. As she continued to scream, I grabbed her; searching for any wound I could find, asking her where she was hurt. She held her heart and pointed to our golden retriever standing just outside the door, with a rabbit in his mouth. Sally gasped, "Just look what Rusty has done now; he's gone and killed the Easter Bunny!" My little girl's heart was broken, and it was time to make very clear the true meaning of Easter, the Resurrection, and the hope we have because of Christ! For years, we continued to color eggs and hide them for the "hunt", but the main focus became the saving grace of the cross.

Both my children were very good at memorizing Bible verses, and it was fun to hear them recite. In her sweet little voice, Sally recited Acts 7:59 to the best of her ability: "An as dey were snoning Sneven, he pwayed, 'Ord Jesus, aceive my pirit, Ord, and do not old nis sin ginst them." Does it get any better than that?

Jay was four when he accepted Jesus into his heart. For a while after his decision, we had a time of finding out just how much he understood about who God is. When my father, who Jay loved very much, passed away, we tried to explain Heaven in response to Jay's questions. I told him that when we die, if we have loved the Lord Jesus with all our hearts and have a relationship with Him, we will be with Jesus forever in Heaven. I explained that was where Grandpa was now, completely healed of his cancer. It was then time to pray before I turned off the light and left the room. Jay's prayer that night was: "Dear Lord Jesus, please come and dead us all so we can be together. Amen". I really thought Jay had accepted death and heaven with an amazing understanding. There were times when I'd find him crying, because he missed Grandpa, but he never questioned God's timing in taking him away. In fact, there were times he even seemed excited about having a grandpa who was with God!

Shortly after the death of my father, my husband decided to take the kids on a trip to see his parents', while I went to spend some time with my mom. He began talking to the kids about all the fun they would have with their grandpa and grandma and uncles, really trying to build up their excitement. Jay started becoming increasingly agitated the more he heard about the trip until one day he just blurted out, "We can't go see Grandpa; he's in heaven and they won't let him out for seven or eight months!" Perhaps this was another throwback to his foster-care days; clearly we needed to find a way to explain heaven isn't like jail; it's everlasting and perfect! I wish I would have recorded more of Jay's prayers. Knowing it would have crushed him to realize I wasn't able to stay as serious as he was in the moment, I spent much of his prayer time biting my tongue to keep from laughing!

After several days with a severe cold and consequently missing all the activities with other kids, he prayed, "Dear God, I'm so tired of this cold. Why don't you take it for a while and we could *share* it. Thanks God. Amen." He could also make a prayer go on forever as he included boats, grandmas, grandpas, and the name of every person he knew. If, after I left the room, he thought of another person, he would just call me back so we could pray all over again.

One evening we were all out for a meal at a restaurant known for its seafood. I was modestly gloating over how well behaved my children were, which should have been the first warning siren to go off in my head. You know the old saying, "Don't count your chickens before they're hatched?" That was me. Jay never missed anything that went on around him, nor did he miss the opportunity to be an informant of anything he deemed important. Unfortunately, a rather large woman caught his interest. As she walked by with her plate of food, Jay said, "Aren't you eating an awful lot for being so fat?" Oh, if looks could kill! Had the table been any larger, I would have crawled underneath. I also considered pretending Jay belonged to someone sitting nearby! Instead, I sat there being the obvious mother of the bold-mouthed, ill-mannered child who had the audacity to say what no doubt others were thinking. Fortunately the woman continued on to her table!

I was blessed to have two children who ate anything I said was good and that was basically everything. I really didn't want them to be finicky children. However, there was a time Jay surprised me. He was around four and the best little shopper, loading the cart with whatever was close enough for him to reach. There were times I'd miss his additions until I was shocked at the check-out counter! On this particular day, he was puzzled by my addition; I bought artichokes to make for dinner. After he'd asked several times what they were, I once again told him they were artichokes and went on to explain I would boil them, dip them in hollandaise sauce and then we'd just eat the tips. Once I'd given this extra information, I told him not to ask again.

That evening, Jay was acting very strange at the dinner table. He would take a bite, then cough or choke. After observing this a few times, I asked him if he liked the artichokes. He burst into tears and said, "Mommy, I just don't want the 'heart to choke' me!" We cleared up the misunderstanding but I felt badly that I hadn't realized all his earlier questions were based on this fear!

Jay also decided to try his hand at shop-lifting. I was furious when I discovered while we were in Safeway, he had "borrowed" a couple of things off their shelf. Fortunately I became aware of this fact when he emptied his pockets in front of me. We marched right back down to the store where he returned his "borrowed" items to the manager. I asked him to please speak to Jay about the consequences of theft, which he did. I thought it had made a real impression, but discovered it only lasted long enough to go in one ear and out the other.

When he was still young, he loved new words and used them every chance he could, sometimes correctly and other times it was anyone's guess what point he was trying to make. One time when he was annoyed with me, he told me so by saying, "Mommy, you make me so fusserated!"

Not long before he turned ten years old, Jay wrote his first song. It was about a bird that had died in spite of Jay's attempt to save it. His tender heart broke and he restricted himself to his room until this song to "Fred" was completed. I smiled at his carefully written manuscript...

> "There was a sparrow named Fred. He lived with me a very short time. He died in 5/15/81. Then we tried to save it by calling the animal doctor. The doctor said try shoving some bread and milk down his throught (throat). But it didn't work, he was dead and I cryied (cried) my head off because he was my only bird I had. Then I beared (buried) him in the backyard by the tree and I said Lord please take this one bird and put it by the side of my grave when I get there. Then when I get up there I will see him. So I can still have a bird named Fred and on his grave up there put this on it, Lord. This is the animal I love so very much so please let him up there because he's done nothing wrong! I love Fred the sparrow."

Both of my children loved to stay with their "Nana." After my father died, Sally usually got to sleep with her. After saying her prayers one evening she asked my mom about the two angel figurines that were sitting on the headboard. Nana explained about God's angels living in heaven and that they also watched over us. After their lengthy conversation, Sally and my mom were just about to sleep when Sally sat up in bed, looked at the angels and said, "What are these again, Nana? Little God-ers?" She had such a funny way of phrasing things. On one cold night, she rolled over to Nana's side of the bed and said, "I'm cold; squish me like the dickens, please!"

Oftentimes when Sally and Jay would stay with my mom they got to explore new foods I rarely had in my kitchen as Nana would buy special treats when she took them shopping. They had just returned from one such outing when Sally asked if she could have "just one freckle, please." Uncertain as to what she was talking about, Mom asked what a freckle was. Sally walked over to the pretzels and repeated, "just one freckle, please." Nana gave her the whole sack!

Another time Sally was helping me clean out a ditch so the water would flow freely. As we were working she asked if I thought God ran around naked or if He wore clothes. I wondered aloud what made her ask that. She said it was such a cold day, she hoped He would ask for clothes if He needed some! My mind was never that inquisitive...ever! Whenever she really wanted to make a point, she'd end her speech by emphatically saying, "And that's no *wie*; that's the *twuth*!" I loved it!

Sally loved to take a bath with me. I would soap up her back, draw pictures on it and she would try to guess what I was drawing. Sometimes I would write a letter she was learning and she would again try to guess what it was. One evening while we were in the tub, we decided to play "follow the leader." I began to copy everything she did, and then it was her turn to copy me. I raised one knee, and she did the same. I moved my left foot, and she did the same. After several times of following me I did something completely different but she didn't catch what I had done. I prompted, "Didn't you see what I did?" Trying to figure it out she replied, "Well, did you *cutted some gas?*"

Another time, Sally, who rarely needed a spanking, was about to get one. For some reason she had taken off all of her clothes (she never just partially undressed), and was standing there waiting for me. I was preparing to spank her when she declared, "Mommy, this is not a spanking bottom!" Amused, I asked "What kind of bottom is it, Sally?" She quickly responded, "It's a kind of bottom to play outside, but it's not a spanking bottom, Mommy!" Remembering "...God's kindness leads you toward repentance..." (Romans 2:4), I decided to show mercy and chose not to spank her. She threw her arms around me and said, "You're my favorite *woman!*" She was four years old!

A few months later, Sally came running into the house yelling for me. When she found me she asked if I knew the difference between and boy and a girl. My mind was moving pretty quickly at that point trying to decide whether she was asking me or about to tell me. Before I could respond, she said, "Well, only girls go *poopie*; boys go *poopie-doo!*" I was learning so much; I wondered how I'd made it that far without such critical information!

She loved to "do" my hair. One very humbling day I would have loved to erase began with Sally asking if she could comb my hair. It was mid-afternoon and I thought what I considered a head massage would feel good, so I said sure. Her next question should have made me think before I answered but I was already so relaxed I may have agreed to most anything. "Mommy, if I give you a beautiful hairdo, will you wear it for the rest of the day?" In hindsight, I should have clarified, "Beautiful to whom?" or perhaps asked for a viewing before I agreed. At the moment I couldn't think of any reason I would need to leave the house, so I assured her, "Of course I'll leave my beautiful hairdo for the rest of the day."

Positively glowing after an additional 45 minutes, she declared she was finished. She could hardly wait for me to see it. As she ushered me into the bathroom she repeated several times how beautiful it was. I'm still not sure how I kept from gasping when I looked in the mirror. There I was with approximately fifty little braids all over my head, each one sporting a different color barrette at the end. I was so thankful I didn't have to leave the house as I congratulated her for her "super imagination" and admired her "skill" in producing such an amazing style all by herself!

I was halfway through our dinner preparations when I discovered I was missing a key ingredient. Realizing I had to go to the store, I went into the bathroom and started to take out the first braid. Sally walked in a minute later and was morti-fied when she saw what I was doing. "Mommy you promised! (Tears began to flow.) You promised you would wear your hair just like I fixed it for the rest of the day!"

Oh my goodness, she was so right, and we'd just recently been talking about the importance of keeping a promise whether you felt like it or not. So, I told Sally she was right, asked for her forgiveness, redid the braid, and together we went to the store. I slinked down the aisle with my head down, hoping I wouldn't see anyone I knew. Sally, on the other hand, walked straight and tall, proudly looking at my hair, so very pleased! My take-away from that day was: If you give your word, you keep it, regardless of the embarrassment it may cause; and, think, *think*, **think** of all the possible consequences of your promise before you give your word!

Sally loved "real school." When she was in third or fourth grade, the children began learning about genetics. The teacher asked all the children to go home and write down the color of their parents' eyes and hair and to also record their height. Sally raised her hand and informed her teacher she didn't know her "real" mom because she was adopted. Her wise and kind teacher immediately responded telling Sally how fortunate she was to be chosen to be someone's daughter. Then, another child in the class raised her hand to say that she, too, was adopted. At that point the teacher put everything aside and let those two little girls answer all kinds of questions the other kids had about adoption. The teacher called me after the class to inform me about what had taken place, expressing his hope that it did not upset me. Not at all! What an amazing day, an entire class period dedicated to adoption, giving two students the honor of experiencing how special they are. When she arrived home, Sally retold the story, including some of the questions she'd been asked. It had clearly been a wonderful day for her.

Writing about Sally reminds me of another day in school that was not quite as wonderful. Sally was in high school when Paul's daughter came to live with us. She was a couple of years younger than Sally, but they got along well. On one occasion, after skipping class, her new sister asked Sally to write a note excusing her absence. She gave Sally the choice of which parent's signature she would copy. Sally's note wasn't questioned by the school secretary, but for *some reason* that same day Sally struggled with a headache. When she went to the office to get an aspirin, Paul happened to walk in right behind her for a totally unrelated visit. In response to the secretary asking what she could do for her, apparently overcome with guilt Sally blurted, "Could I please have a nervous?" We actually didn't find out about the forged note for years, but Sally thought for sure that was why Paul had shown up at the school! I love how God's "coincidences" work!

I need to tell one more story about Sally when she was fourteen years old. Let me preface it by saying I thought all kids wanted to drive, probably because I was taught to drive very early and loved it. Well, my daughter was not me and certainly had not great ambitions of getting behind the wheel of a car. I took her out into the country on a lovely afternoon, pulled the car over to the side of the gravel road and got into the back seat. I told her we could go home when she decided to take us there. I still chuckle when I remember all the pleading and begging that I would not make her drive met by my own determination that she would. One minor detail was that the car was a 4-speed, manual shift. After a few tears and much negotiating, she finally got into the driver's seat. The clutch only gave her a few problems, mainly in first gear, but it wasn't long before we were cruising down the road and made it home in one piece. She ground the gears often, but I didn't think it was the time to complain since it would only give her another reason to avoid driving.

Once she got her driver's permit, I made her drive a lot. Sunday morning she was taking me to church and had stopped to wait for a car before crossing traffic to turn into the parking lot. I'm not sure why, but at the very last minute she decided to go ahead and turn before the car passed. Startled beyond reason, I am absolutely positive my eyes have never been that big since! Having frightened herself as well, my precious daughter let out an expletive. Her exclamation shocked us both as much as the turn had and I couldn't help but laugh! I concluded if it was ever right to swear, that seemed like the time to do it…in the church parking lot, heading into the service, after narrowly escaping being broadsided by an oncoming vehicle! She did turn out to be a good driver, but it still isn't her favorite thing to do. I, on the other hand, drive to relax!

Chapter 9

Illnesses & Accidents

Psalm 6:9 "The Lord has heard my cry for mercy; the Lord accepts my prayer..."

I think one of the greatest challenges a parent has to deal with is a sick child. Now I am fine with just about anything as long as my child, or anyone else for that matter, does not throw up. Unfortunately, as soon as I'm exposed to that part of sickness, I tend to join them. Fortunately, my two children seldom threw up! But they did have some doozie illnesses.

One morning I went to waken Jay and discovered he was in a world of his own. Realizing he was delirious, I called the hospital to ask what I should do. They advised me to bring him right in to the emergency room. Since he was still very young, they took him to a pediatric exam room that happened to be covered with wallpaper of hippopotamuses every size and color. Trying to keep Jay awake, I asked him what they all had in common. He told me they were all fat, but they were all different colors. About that time, a large, very over-weight nurse stepped into the room and Jay who was so, so sick looked at her and said, "Mom, is she, a nurse-apotamus?" I cringed and sank into the chair. I think I was actually getting used to being put in the hot seat by my son, though he was almost always oblivious to it.

When a known "childhood disease" was going around the area, the school district where we were living had a unique policy. The district representative called each family that had children registered for the following year, inviting them to participate in a school sponsored play-day at the gym with the sick kids. It was their hope that everyone would be exposed at once rather than have the illness drag on for months throughout the school year. This particular time the "invitation" went out for chicken pox exposure. Though Jay spent many hours playing in a gym full of sick kids, several of whom were quite 'spotted,' but he never came down with them.

Consequently, when we moved the following year and discovered chicken pox was once again the disease going around I wasn't the least bit concerned. Since Jay had already been 'super' exposed with no outbreak, I was quite surprised when he wakened one morning, looking like a spotted hen. His fever climbed to over 104 degrees. The next night, he fell out of bed and didn't have the strength to get up off the floor. A couple days later, I became very sick with the flu and was too weak myself to care for Jay. My husband had to stay home from work the whole week, taking over the household chores, plus caring for Sally, Jay and myself. During that time I found Jay lying on the floor beside the door, having attempted to crawl to the bathroom. I broke into tears; we were both so exhausted. He didn't even have the energy to call out for help. Yet, just one week later, Jay came running into our room at 5:30 am. He felt great, announcing he was hungry, and ready to take his bath before going to school! We were thankful for all three, but not before 7 am.

When Sally was quite young, she fell out of her swing. The next day I noticed a weird swelling on the back of her head. During his examination a couple hours later, the doctor confirmed she had something lodged under her skin. He laid her up on the table, injected a numbing medication, and sure enough, as he was "blowing up" her skin, out popped a rock. Throughout the whole appointment, she never cried once, just laid there completely still. Both the doctor and I were amazed at her composure. She proudly kept the small rock.

Neither of my children seemed to mind shots. I, on the other hand, will avoid them if there is any way possible. We could go to the doctor's office and both Jay and Sally would have their sleeves rolled up before we even went into the exam room. I will never forget when we all had to go in for poison oak shots. (I'm still not sure why!) The doctor thought it would be a good idea for me to set an example for the children, to show them it wouldn't hurt. Who are you kidding? It hurt! But because I had four eyes glued to my face anticipating a very brave mother, I had to become one very brave mother. I don't suggest this. The needle *really* hurt; I winced while trying to smile, and my children laughed. When it was their turn, they each took their shot like it was no big deal and went home happy to play. What was wrong with them? That just isn't normal!

One day that all changed for Jay. He was already sitting in the chair waiting for the nurse to stick his arm with the needle, when another nurse walked in the room. She caught Jay's attention and he turned to look at her just as the other nurse poked Jay's arm. The movement was just enough to break the needle, leaving it in his arm. By the time the nurse was able, with help, to "dig" the needle out of his arm, Jay had determined that was the last shot he would ever have. From then on, it took at least two professionals to hold him down. I didn't blame him and let him kick and scream all he wanted. It broke my heart.

Although both my children liked to climb everything in sight, it was a challenge to keep my eye on Sally. At age 7, one of her favorite things was to climb the fir tree we had in our backyard. She loved to climb to the very top and then get the tree to sway as she held on tightly. On one of those occasions, as she was climbing down, her foot slipped and she crashed through the branches. By the time she finally hit the ground, she had knocked out her two front teeth. I heard her screaming, ran outside, was relieved to find no broken bones, but then she handed me her teeth. I shoved them back in her mouth and we headed for the dentist. He didn't think we would be able to save them but decided to give it a try. After cementing them together, he sent us home. The following week I got a call from the school telling me Sally and another little girl had collided while jumping rope and that her front teeth were out. I asked them to put them back in, then I jumped in my car. Once again we were at the dentist and this time he cemented the back side of the teeth all the way across, telling us again there was little chance they could be saved. As an adult, Sally still sports those same front teeth, just another miracle from our amazing God!

At age 13, Sally had a growth on her head. To eliminate ongoing concerns, we went to see the doctor. He felt it should be removed and planned to do it the next week. Sally is probably the bravest young lady I've ever known and faces just about everything with confidence. When she went in for her surgery, I went in with her. The doctor deadened the area on her head and once sure she was numb, he began to cut out the area of concern. I was watching and happened to glance down at Sally's face to see tears running down her cheeks. I asked her if she could feel the knife and she said yes! The tears began to run down my face and the doctor felt terrible, wishing he had known sooner. He stopped and gave her another injection before continuing the surgery. She never would have said anything but would have stayed absolutely still regardless of the pain!

I had already seen her bravery earlier in her life when she would take the blame for something Jay had done, just to keep him from getting into trouble. Even when we knew the punishment belonged to Jay, Sally would beg us to give it to her. She had such a heart for her brother, so much love, and hated seeing him get grounded, or any other kind of discipline. Now I had witnessed another example of her bravery in the area of physical pain.

Chapter 10

Moving Again

*Psalm 4:1 "...Give me relief from my distress;
be merciful to me and hear my prayer."*

I went through the motions of saying good-bye: sitting on the deck of our home, inhaling the wonderfully fresh air, looking out over the valley, walking in the garden, digging my toes into the dirt, looking for our "pet" snake, and allowed the tears to run down my face. We were moving. I loved where we were, but some things did not fit our needs and my husband took another job. Our children were getting older, well, not really older, but they were growing up. We wanted to get them into good schools; we were ready to meet new people and make new friends.

Sally was enrolled in kindergarten and Jay was ready to start second grade. While we were between homes, the children and I stayed with my mother. Early in the morning, Sally, who was sleeping with my mom, woke up, took my mother's hands in hers and said, "Look, we both have wrinkly hands in the morning!" Mom couldn't find the wrinkles on Sally's hands, just her own!

We moved into a house outside of town with lots of room for the kids to run, and run they did. Both of them could be occupied just with their imaginations; I loved to watch them play. Our animal collection was pared down to two golden retriever puppies and two hamsters; sadly, "our" garden snake did not come with us. The end of our summer was spent moving in, getting to know our neighbors, finding a church, and becoming acquainted with the town.

I was very pleased with the schools and both Jay and Sally were anxious to meet new kids. September 27, 1979, shortly after school had resumed, I got a phone call from Jay's teacher. She quickly summed up the reason for her call telling me that Jay, while standing in line to check out a ball for recess, had bitten another boy in the stomach. I immediately sent up a prayer, "Oh Lord, You'd better rescue me; I'm out of resources!"

Situation after situation began to happen in rapid succession and I was at my wits end. I noticed more than ever, in Jay's mind, he was never to blame. His reasoning most often bordered on the bizarre I was becoming so stretched in how to handle him that there were times I wanted to crawl into a closet and just stay there. One morning I noticed my paring knife was missing from the kitchen. By now my mind immediately suspected Jay for taking just about anything that wasn't where it should be. This was no exception. I checked his room, and there it was. He'd been using it to carve on his window sill. I didn't know where he came up with these ideas!

I was so mad; I confined him to his room so I wouldn't lose control. Why couldn't he have carved a bar of soap, or a piece of wood like other kids? I told him to stay in his room with the door closed, until I told him to come out. I finished getting Sally ready for school and sent her out to catch the bus. As I was beginning to calm down, the phone rang. It was the school counselor asking me if I was all right. "Of course," I responded, "I'm just fine." It was the next question that shed a little light on the call. The counselor asked, "Is Jay all right?" Surprised, I responded, "Why do you ask?" The counselor then told me that when he didn't see Jay get off the bus, he asked Sally if Jay was sick. She answered, "No, Jay's in his bedroom where mom can't kill him!" The counselor then asked me, "Would you mind if I came over?" It was clear there was only one correct answer! I was quite certain if I'd said 'no,' the police would have been the counselor's next call! I sweetly said, "Of course not." The school counselor came over with the psychiatrist and asked right away if they could please see Jay. If they would have just stopped to listen, they could have heard Jay singing away in his room. He wasn't being punished, I WAS! Once they saw Jay and saw that he was as happy as ever, things settled down and clearly in their minds I became an okay parent once again.

Truthfully, as I look back, there were times I felt like my sanity *was* at stake. I wonder how many other moms were going through trials; I wish we could have met. As for Jay, my fears were mounting. I knew something was off, very, very off. He continued to have a sensitive, wonderful heart, but no ownership of wrong doing. I had never witnessed anything like this in children before and felt like sinkholes were appearing faster than I could fill them.

Our new town had a river that ran through it and Jay loved to fish. At bedtime one evening, his dad promised Jay that whenever he woke up, they could go fishing. At 3:30 am, Jay was ready to go, and they did.

In the midst of all the challenges Jay provided, Sally was growing into a responsible little girl, ready to take on the chores healthy for all children to learn. We started with learning how to set the table, then progressed to carrying her laundry down to the basket, and feeding the animals. The newness of this developmental stage wore off quickly. One evening, she was sitting at the table coloring as I was fixing dinner. I asked her to please help me set the table. She crossed her arms, looked right at me, and asked, "Now tell me, when does one have time to just relax and sit in the living room?" Holding back a smile, I told her we could discuss that later but now she needed to set the table!

A few years later, when Sally was around twelve, she came home with a really bad attitude. Deciding she needed some extra sleep, I told her she would be going to bed early that night. She concluded this was my problem and apparently I must be angry. She asked, "Why are you mad?" I told her I wasn't. Sally tried again, "I am just sure you're on the verge of yelling!" Confusing her further, I calmly asked, "Why do you say that, Sally? *I'm* not yelling." Sally, confirming her need for more sleep, started crying and gasped, "I don't know! It just seems like the verge should be close now!" We had obviously entered the delightful, female pre-adolescent stage...and she thought *I* was on "*the verge*?" Yes, definitely...communication at its finest!

We loved Christmas, wintertime, and snow!

Chapter 11

Reality

Psalm 34:18 "The Lord is close to the bro-
kenhearted and saves those who are crushed
in spirit."

As time went on, more and more bizarre and unusual things began to happen. For example, Jay painted a portion of the neighbor's house using my makeup. He didn't like the color they had and, in his words, "…thought shades of brown would look much better. I wanted them to see it with their own eyes!" Fortunately, we had wonderful neighbors and Jay's only punishment was to wash the side of their house. He never could understand why. It was so obvious to him it had improved the color.

Sally became even more protective of him. He was so sharp, and yet I noticed he had absolutely no common sense. One evening, after he had shop-lifted something from the store, I found the item. Since we had been through this before with the Safeway incident, this time I called the police and asked them to please talk with him. They were wonderful. The police came over and spent quite a bit of time going over the process of an arrest for someone caught stealing. They listed the consequences of having a record, and the damage done to one's reputation. Again, I hoped it would affect Jay's thinking, and it actually seemed to for a day or two, but that was about all.

My marriage started to flounder under the continual pressure of ongoing disagreements; we were constantly arguing about how to deal with our son. Tension grew as Jay dominated our time, while Sally was left in the shadows. I didn't know how to change things. I tried taking Sally away for a special week-end, but it seemed to evaporate when we returned to the same atmosphere we'd left. I was continually awed by Sally's love for Jay; it seemed when Jay was being punished, Sally felt it as well.

Looking for healthy outlets, we signed Jay up for various sports. He was a natural and loved every activity, running, throwing balls, etcetera, so we taught him how to play tennis, baseball, basketball, anything that was offered. While he was involved in a sport, life was almost normal. Sally also expressed interest and started playing softball at the same time. As good as it was for the children, the schedule was crazy for us! We found ourselves running between fields in order to catch at least half of each game. Then, one day on the football field at school, Jay had a seizure.

Our local doctor sent us up to the Oregon Health Sciences University in Portland, OR. Jay underwent many tests and one of the results showed his brain was unable to make any quick change from light to dark, or dark to light. That day on the football field, he had looked into the sun and his brain waves couldn't keep up with the change in light. Additionally, for the first time, we were also told that Jay's entire nervous system was damaged from the drugs his mother had used while she was pregnant.

He was diagnosed as having Fetal Drug and Alcohol syndrome, which meant he was born without the ability to use common sense. There were almost weekly trips to Portland for many tests, though none reported anything encouraging. Our son had been born with irreversible damage to his Central Nervous System. This was who he was and that was how he would spend the rest of his life. Though this information provided the pieces of the puzzle we'd been missing, my heart ached; nothing was going to change. I admit I couldn't grasp the permanence of it. Here was a young boy whose life had been totally stolen from him by an utterly selfish woman wanting drugs and sex, with no regard for her baby. I still find myself angry at such unnecessary and selfish behavior. It seems like women who choose drugs and alcohol should have their tubes tied before being allowed to harm their children. How can there be no remorse in killing a baby, or bringing drug babies into our world?

**Jay was a natural athlete; his coordination was amazing.
Fishing was the perfect exercise for his patience, or lack thereof.**

Our dogs enjoyed the job of protecting the children!

Just another rainy day to enjoy!

Sally and Jay were very tender with the animals.

Chapter 12

Answered Prayer

Psalm 32:7 "You are my hiding place, You will protect me from trouble and surround me with songs of deliverance."

Jay's father and I ended our marriage after 12 years. It was decided Jay would live with his father; life was a struggle for both of them right up to the end. Money and other items started "disappearing." Jay's lies became his "norm;" I'm not even sure he knew when he was lying! He got into trouble more and more frequently. Keeping him involved no longer helped; things just went from bad to worse. Jay was put into a home for troubled kids in Alaska and then was eventually sent to a behavior modification home and school in Portland, Oregon. I visited him often, met with the counseling staff and many times brought him home for the weekend.

We were hopeful at times of seeming improvement, but then it would all collapse. There were times when his home visits were wonderful and other times when I would count the hours until I could take him back. I never knew when he'd stolen something from me until I'd get a phone call from the home after they had found something in his suitcase. My emotions were torn and the guilt of anticipating the worst would at times consume me. I longed for some sort of normality. I know Jay did as well. He remained there until he was 18.

Jay would come home for week-end visits.
It was always a time of concern.

**Looking at pictures of Jay one would never guess
the turmoil going on inside.**

It was five years later that I met and married Paul. He was a firefighter in Portland, his sister introduced us. I was 36 at the time. On our second date, Sally and I met him for dinner at a restaurant in Salem. As we were eating, Paul commented that he didn't know how old I was. Before I could answer, Sally said, "She's forty." I retorted, "I am not 40; I'm 36!" Sally teased further, "You always say that mom, but you know you're 40." Paul listened to our back-and-forth conversation, then finally asked, "May I see your driver's license?" Looking at my license and realizing Sally's wit, he looked at her and smiled, "Sally, I like you; we're going to get along very well!" We married a few months later.

One of the first things Paul did was sit down with Sally and discuss his role in our new family. He asked if he could take the first six months for the two of them to get acquainted before he stepped into full head of our home. He took Sally on regular dates to the bowling alley, ice cream shop, church functions and ball games. I was in awe of his wisdom and sat back watching the bond grow between the two of them. At the end of the six months, they reevaluated. This time Paul asked Sally if she was ready for him to become the head of the entire house. Sally was ready to accept Paul unconditionally. Their bond continues to this day. How blessed I am. As wonderful as it was to be married, we both brought emotional baggage with us. Having a son like Jay would prove to be a challenge. It was nice to have Paul comfort me in some of the more trying times. As trouble with Jay increased, so did Paul's concerns. His schedule as a firefighter involved regular time away from home and his experience in dealing with the issues increased his apprehension. After more issues with Jay involving drugs and other addicts, I put a restraining order on Jay in order to protect Sally and myself.

Once Jay was out of the completely controlled environment at the school, he began using drugs, drinking, and living a life of no responsibility. He would steal from people and then call me when put into prison. In his mind, it was always the other person's fault. One time he was caught going out the window with a television. His explanation was, the TV belonged to the guy he was with but because the door was

locked, they had to enter through the window. When I asked
him why they didn't exit through the door, he said it was still
locked and they couldn't find the key.

Another time, he told me that the person they were stealing
from had too much anyway and it was wrong for someone to
have so much. When I asked him why he thought the person
was so prosperous in the first place, Jay couldn't give me an
answer. I suggested that maybe he had worked and saved
his money to buy the things he owned. Jay argued with that,
saying he didn't have to make so much money.

On rare occasions Jay would get a job. He was hired at
the dam to be a laborer and asked me if I would help him buy
some clothes. I went to Portland and bought him new work
boots, pants, shirts, and a coat. One week later, the motel
where he'd been staying called to say Jay hadn't returned.
They wanted to know what to do with the nice clothes he'd
left behind. I had them donated to the Salvation Army. That
was the last time I bought Jay anything other than lunch
or dinner.

When he would call home, I never knew what stories to
believe. At times he'd tell me he was living under a bridge,
or with "people," or say he was renting a home. One time he
called to say he'd gotten married, even gave me a name, but
there was nothing in the registry when I checked. He could
never give me an address where he was living. When I went
to see him, we'd meet in downtown Portland.

His calls were very sporadic; sometimes it would be weeks between calls, then it stretched into months, and at one point became a year in between calls. I honestly didn't know if he was dead or alive. When he was arrested for something or caught in the act, it would precipitate a call. I remember one call was more bizarre than others, when we ended up in a very political conversation, oddly enough. He said he was planning on suing the prison for not meeting his needs. I asked him why he would want to sue me? He just laughed and said he wasn't suing me, he was suing the prison. I asked him where he thought the prison money came from if not from my pocket through taxes. He had never thought of that! By the end of the conversation, having explained to him that even his "free housing and meals" were paid for by me and people like me, he decided he would forego the lawsuit. I said "Great, maybe my taxes won't go up again this year!" Of course, I knew *that* was a joke!

One afternoon my mother got a call from Jay when he was high on drugs. He told my mom he was at my house talking with me. His voice was scaring my mom as his conversation became increasingly inappropriate. When mom asked if she could talk with me, he said no because I had fallen asleep. Mom could tell something wasn't right and told Jay she had to go. She immediately called the police in my town. I'd actually been away from the house at the time of Jay's call to my mother, but when I approached my home just a few minutes later I saw that it was surrounded by several policemen. After checking my identification, they asked if I knew where my son was, and when I had last seen him. My house was thoroughly searched before I was allowed to go in. As previously mentioned, I already had a restraining order on Jay, so they were perhaps even more vigilant.

Another home visit

When I confronted Jay with what had happened, he denied it completely. He had no recall at all. At that time we still had Sally and also Paul's daughter living in our home. From that point on, my family members agreed not to take any more of Jay's calls. It seemed he was getting further and further away from any kind of healthy reality. I spent a lot of time on my knees praying and had many other people praying for my son as well. I often asked God why he chose me to be

Jay's mother when I felt so helpless. But as I look back, I'm thankful He gave us the opportunity to introduce Him to Jay, through our prayer times and Bible stories at home, through going to Sunday school and church, and through our friends. God knew Jay.

From then on, Jay usually called home when he was in prison. Sally and I went to visit him one time when he was in a prison nearby. The whole event was quite an experience. First, we were told that Sally's clothes were not acceptable; there was a dress-code for visitors. We left and went shopping for some other pants, found a cheap pair, and headed back to the prison. Then, as we got out of our car and started walking toward the entrance, we heard a voice over the loud speaker saying, "Get on the sidewalk." We had no idea who they were speaking to, so we kept walking. Again we heard, "Get on the sidewalk." We kept walking. Once again the loud speaker came on and said, "You two women walking toward the prison entrance, I will not tell you again, get on the sidewalk." That was the first time we realized he was talking to us! Realizing *we* were the "two women," we immediately got on the sidewalk. Next, we had to go through the scanner without setting off the alarm. Not aware it was a metal detector, we did set it off! After removing our shoes, belts, and outer garments, we finally passed! This was all new and very foreign. At last we were sent into the visiting room and Jay entered. We couldn't hug him or sit by him, but we did have a good visit. He was so jovial and upbeat, you never would have known he was in a prison. All around us were men of every age and it broke my heart to see so many with young children who came to visit, broken families, broken children and hurting, broken mothers. Some of the teens in the visiting area had already taken on a hardened appearance, likely defending the hurt they had inside. I wondered about their future and just had to ask God to please save those sitting around me. "Just place someone or something in their lives that would direct them to know You love them, as they are, in their circumstances. Please give them hope."

On July 8th, 2006, I got a phone call telling me Jay had passed away. My heart sank as I wondered where my son was at that very moment. I had prayed for so many years that he would be healed and that God would not let him die alone. I expected God to answer my prayers. I had to make a decision regarding Jay's body and burial. I was given a number to call, not aware the Lord was about to lead me into an experience full of peace and greater spiritual excitement than I'd had in a very long time.

Chapter 13

Jay's Final Chapter of Grace

"God will wipe away every tear from their eyes; there shall be no more death, nor sorrow, nor crying. There shall be no more pain, for the former things have passed away. He who sat on the throne said, 'Behold, I make all things new.'" Revelation 21:4-5

Two weeks prior to Jay's death, he had finally had enough of the lifestyle he was living. Unable to change by himself, he sought out a Christian ranch for drug addicts located in southern Washington. The couple who ran the camp called it, "Mountain Ministries." Jay arrived by himself and checked in, declaring he wanted his life from that point on to be lived for God, not for himself. The rules of the camp were very strict. There would be no drugs, no drinking, no smoking, and no contact with anyone on the "outside" for two full weeks. Committed to change, Jay went cold-turkey, giving up drinking, smoking, and drugs. Under supervision, he helped maintain the grounds at a local church, attended Bible studies, participated in prayer groups and obeyed every rule to reach his goal. His 37th birthday was spent hiking to the top of a hill and celebrating with a group of men who shared his new goal of "life change." A few days later, he was sitting in a Bible study when he started to feel sick and excused himself to go use the restroom. There he had a seizure, hit his head, and died immediately, going directly into the arms of Jesus!

Sally and I drove to Mountain Ministries to hear the story of his final days. He would have been allowed to call home the day after he died. I never got to meet the "new and changed" Jay, but praise God we did get to hear the most wonderful stories about his changed life. Many of the men there shared things that made my heart sing.

The wonderful lady who, with her husband, ran the camp said she wanted to share something with Sally and me. She took us to her refrigerator and showed us two lists of names, one on the left side, and one on the right side. She explained that the names on the right had not yet reached their goals but were working to change their lives. The names on the left side had graduated from the camp because their goals had been met and they were able to leave and function on their own. Then she asked me to note which side held Jay's name. He was on the left; he had graduated! He not only graduated from the camp, he graduated into the arms of his Savior, the Lord Jesus Christ. My son was Home; he was completely healed;

he was whole. When God answered my prayers, He went far beyond my expectations, and the joy has never left me.

When I hear someone tell me they're sorry to hear my son died, I assure them they don't need to be, because Jay certainly isn't! He wouldn't want it any different and neither would I! Sally and I occasionally talk about Jay, all that we learned from him, how unfair life can sometimes be, the hurt that was caused, but also remember the humor he brought to our lives. We choose to remember *his smile!* God honored my prayers; Jay was surrounded by people who truly cared for and loved him when he passed from this life. I am so grateful.

**This is the last picture we have of Jay,
taken just two days before his death.**

In the aftermath of his death, I had another wonderful surprise as our lives were settling down. The choir I direct at our church is filled with amazing hearts that surpass even their musical talent. Though only one of them had ever met Jay, they all came up to my home bringing dinner and we shared the most incredible celebration honoring my son. The support they showed to me was beyond anything I have ever experienced. At one point, they were standing outside and singing when my phone rang. One of the neighbors on the hill over from our house said, "I don't have a clue what's going on at your place, but tell them not to stop. The music is beautiful!" And it was.

The choir had gone together and gifted me with a beautiful stone bench. My husband later built a pergola to place it in. It is a wonderful reminder of God's miracle. We picked out a blooming tree to go beside it, originally planning to place Jay's ashes in the hole as we planted it. Not too surprising for me, when it came time to plant I forgot the ashes.

Several years after Jay's death, the sun was out, the hummingbirds were making a lot of noise, the robins were in the bird bath and it was nearly a perfect day. When I looked out my dining room window I could see Jay's tree in full bloom with the sun spotlighting the blossoms. I knew it was time to put his ashes where they belonged. There was not a trace of wind and my mind was just flowing with memories of my children playing tag in the yard and climbing trees. Jay's ashes had been sitting on a shelf too long. I took them out to his tree and slowly placed them all around the base. They were absolutely perfect ashes and a surreal sense of peace completely washed over me. This may not make sense, but this final step took place exactly when it should. I sang a few songs and let the peace of God consume me.

Later that day, when my husband came home, I walked out to the shop where he was welding on a project. Though I know it's hard to stop in the middle of a project, he took off his helmet when he saw me and met me half way. I told him I'd buried Jay that day, and he simply put his arms around me and held me. His response could not have been more appropriate, and I'm so grateful for this man I married. That season of our lives was finally put to rest. My son is not ashes, he is a living being absorbing his Heavenly Father's beauty. He is laughing, and he is whole. What a gift we have waiting for us! It seems like the peace in my heart expands even more every spring when I see the beautiful new blossoms.

Sally is now a mother of two grown children and I am amazed at the amount of patience she had with them growing up. I know she must have thought about our lives with Jay as she raised them. Her heart for her brother was endless love. She has the same for her children.

We've often talked about wishing both of her children could have known a healthy Jay. They would have loved him because Jay loved kids. His heart was huge, yet his mind had been stripped by the drugs of his birth mother. What he wanted and what he could give were at opposite ends of the spectrum. I can only imagine what his potential would've been, given a normal life. I will always remember his forgiving nature, his ability to see the best in someone, his desire for the approval of others and his outgoing personality. What an experience. And, someday, I will get to see Jay exactly as God intended him to be... *perfect*!

Chapter 14

Limited Understanding Mingled with Mercy

I am so thankful for the Lord's sovereignty and unsurpassable wisdom. I know I'm a grateful recipient of His daily compassion and mercy, which Lamentations 3 tells us are renewed every morning. Throughout the majority of this book, I've shared many of the challenging experiences of raising my drug baby; through all of it I realize that judgment belongs to the only One who judges righteously. I fully embrace the truth of *James 2:13 "...Mercy triumphs over judgment."*

However, in my limited frame of reference this side of heaven, it's very difficult for me to understand why young women keep a baby when they're not able or willing to give that child the appropriate place of priority in their lives? What kind of selfish generations are we raising? I do not express these thoughts lightly because in addition to adopting a child, I've also wrestled with the difficult decisions a birth mother faces.

I became pregnant at seventeen. There was never a moment that I thought about abortion. This was my error, not the baby's. I spent a lot of time weighing the pros and cons of keeping that little baby when it arrived. I pondered many questions such as: Was I mature enough to raise a baby without a completed education? Was I willing and able to give up the next eighteen years of my life to meet this child's needs? Was it best for the child to have only a mother and not a father? Was I so prideful to think I could do a better job than someone else? As much as I tried to justify answers to my questions, I knew it would not be best for my baby to keep her.

I was also convinced that another wrong choice, specifically abortion, would only make matters worse, not better. My parents were wonderful people ready to support me in whatever decision I made. I struggled with all the thoughts any mother-to-be imagines. What would my baby look like? Would this child share my passion for music and sports? Would he or she have a great sense of humor like the members of my family? Would he or she hate me for choosing to give them up for adoption? Would I ever have the chance to meet my baby if I did?

I was often haunted at night with these thoughts and the stupid, awful sin I had committed. My choices never affected just me, they followed the ripple effect and everyone surrounding me was pulled into the drama. My little sister, big brother, parents, on and on and on. If only I'd been wise enough to think beyond myself and the moment; if only I'd trusted that my parents knew more than I did; if only...

I chose to give my little baby life with a complete family, a father and a mother who could nurture all the areas a child needs. My heart broke over and over the day my little girl was born. I chose not to meet her that day, because I knew if I held her, I would decide to keep her out of sheer selfishness. So she went home with another family and was raised without any input from me. Since this story is not ultimately about her, I will simply say that fifteen years later we did meet and the Lord has given us a wonderful relationship. We were able to work through her many questions, some of which were very hard to answer, but the friendship we now have was worth all the effort it took to heal. Though I'd stepped out of God's will at the time of her conception, He blessed me as I returned to Him.

I wish those who've chosen to be repeatedly promiscuous would simply have their tubes tied. What a simple procedure that would prevent the unwanted from being born and prevent the abortion industry from making a fortune by killing babies. It would also prevent children from being born with permanent drug or alcohol damage to their bodies, as in Jay's case. I just wonder how much further our society will deteriorate before the Lord Jesus Christ returns.

While writing this book, I had an enlightening conversation with my dear, literally life-long friend, Trudy. I asked if she'd like to read what I'd written before I sought to have it published. Not only did she say yes, she shared an insightful thought that thrilled my heart then and now. "You do realize that although Jay is not here to give his testimony of how God worked in his life, you are giving it for him. You are Jay's mouthpiece!" Trudy's comment made my spirit soar!

Hindsight gives us the ability to glimpse the good outcome God had planned all along. Although there are other things I know I will never understand while here on earth, it really doesn't matter. "God is good, all the time; all the time, God is good." Over the years I've had the opportunity to talk to many mothers about losing a child, or those with a child who seems to be going down a very negative path of their own choosing. I can always go back to Jay's story, and encourage others with the truth that we never know how the story's going to end until it's over. We do not give up hope, we do not despair, we pray, we pray, and we pray.

We need to remind ourselves that our children are truly just a gift given to us for an unknown period of time, and we need to make the most of what we have because any time is better than none! We have to do our best to complete the purpose for which God has given them to us. I have to admit there were times I didn't feel like doing His work. Knowing my own inadequacies, I questioned being Jay's mom. But looking back, it is so different. I hope, when I enter heaven and hold Jay, he can say to me, "Thank you Mom. You introduced me to God and we have an amazing relationship!"

And, I believe when God holds me, He will say, "You were chosen to be Jay's mom. Jay was *never* an *accident* placed in your care."

If only we could all see from the future, looking back, but we can't, so let me tell you, hold fast to what you know is right; it's worth it and you will be greatly rewarded for your faithfulness.

> *"Let us not become weary in doing good, for*
> *at the proper time we will reap a harvest if we*
> *do not give up." Galatians 6:9*

I do have one piece of advice to add for parents going through difficult times with their children. I've learned how important it is to let your children experience the consequences for the choices they make. Our children can never know who God is as long as we are rescuing them. In doing so, we become their god, the one they call for help, the one who bails them out of their trouble, the one who gives them money to replace the money they wasted. Often, it's only when they hit rock bottom that their need for the real God is fully evident. Then, when the cry for help is going upward, He can respond and fill them with His love, ~~mercy,~~ power, and grace.

I am now in my 60's and life has flown by. Today my husband and I enjoy our grandchildren; we have such great times with them! They've learned to "tube" with us and always enjoy daring Paul to dump them in the river. I'm still an avid camera buff and both grandchildren cooperate with my "photo shoots;" I absolutely love having their pictures on our walls! They've grown up helping us in the yard, occasionally driving the tractor, most often laughing together. They've rafted the river with Paul while I drove from bridge to bridge to get pictures of them going through the rapids, always hoping they wouldn't overturn. They're game for just about anything and everything. They keep us young, and bring us such encouragement for the next generation.

Sally is a wonderful daughter, quite content with having been adopted. She's never had the desire to seek out her birth mom, as Jay did. I must admit that's been a real relief to me. I never think of her as *adopted*. I know we both forget she is, and I think that's the way it should be. No one could love her any more than we do, and it brings us joy that she is confident of our steadfast love.

**I'm grateful for the many happy memories we were
able to capture in pictures.**

Sally, me and Paul... life has been, and continues to be good.

Epilogue

enjoy sitting down with most of my old memories and others I wish I could redo. Thankfully, I have a Heavenly Father who's forgiven me for my failures and keeps me looking forward to Him. What a day it will be when I go to my permanent home. Until then, I plan to continue experiencing His daily blessings of laughter, family, and friends. I love this life. I can only imagine how much greater it will be in His presence, with the awesome excitement of meeting God face-to-face, being with my family members already there, and meeting my changed son. Goosebumps stand on my arms as I anticipate this!

Thank you for reading my story and now, take the time to start yours. We all need to learn and be encouraged by one another! To that end, I would love to hear from any of my readers. You may reach me through LessonsInGrace@gmail.com

"Be anxious for nothing, but in everything by
prayer and supplication with thanksgiving,

let your requests be made known to God; and the peace of God, which surpasses all understanding, will guard your hearts and minds through Christ Jesus. Finally brethren, whatever things are true, whatever things are noble, whatever things are just, whatever things are pure, whatever things are lovely, whatever things are of good report, if there is any virtue and if there is anything praiseworthy, meditate on these things." Phillippians 4:0-8

CPSIA information can be obtained
at www.ICGtesting.com
Printed in the USA
FSOW02n1206311017
40580FS

9 781498 476928